Introduction

The captain gave Claggart a cold look. "Is your story true?" he asked. "Be careful. If you're lying, I'll have to punish you."

Claggart shook his head sadly. "I'm sorry, sir, it's true," he said. "And I can prove it."

Captain Vere looked into Claggart's eyes, then turned away. "Can he prove it?" he asked himself. "What can I do?" He decided to talk to Billy Budd.

He wanted to do this quietly. He didn't want the other men on the ship to know about this problem. The other officers were watching him as he talked to Claggart.

What is true and what is a lie? Who is good and who is bad? What is right and what is wrong? The people in this story have to ask themselves these questions.

The year is 1797. Billy Budd is a young English sailor who is working on a merchant ship. But the King needs more sailors. A Navy officer comes and takes Billy onto a warship. Billy did not choose to join the Navy, but he is not unhappy about the change.

Billy is handsome and friendly, so everyone on the warship likes him. He does his work well, and he always helps the other men. He is honest and good, but he makes an enemy, John Claggart.

Claggart is the opposite of Billy, and he hates him. He wants to be like Billy, but he can't. Maybe, too, he has feelings for Billy that many people will not understand. Claggart makes trouble for Billy, and the result is a serious problem on the ship.

Captain Vere is an honest man, and he wants to do the right thing. But he has to choose between his feelings and the law. He is a captain in the King's Navy. He asks the opinion of his officers, but he has to think about his ship. In the end, he has to decide.

At that time, life was difficult in the Navy. The men worked hard on the ships, and they had to obey the orders of the captain and the officers. In 1797, many English sailors refused to obey these orders. They wanted the Navy to make their lives easier. There were a number of mutinies, and some things changed, but many men were punished.

After these mutinies, the captains watched the sailors carefully for signs of trouble. They punished men who did not obey orders. We must remember that, at this time, England was at war with France.

Billy Budd, Sailor was Herman Melville's last book. Melville was born in New York City in 1819. His father died when he was 12, and he worked in a bank and then in his brother's store. He later worked as a cabin boy on a ship to Liverpool.

When he was twenty-one, he went to sea on a fishing boat. After eighteen months, he left the ship in the Pacific Islands. He traveled to Hawaii, and he returned to Boston on an American naval ship.

He left the Navy in 1844 and wrote popular books about his adventures. *Typee* (1846) and *Omoo* (1847) were stories about the Pacific Islands. In 1851, he wrote *Redburn, His First Voyage*. In this story, a young man travels on a ship for the first time. *White-Jacket* (1850) is a story about life in the Navy.

Melville married and moved to a farm in Massachusetts in 1850. The writer Nathaniel Hawthorne was one of his neighbors.

Melville wrote *Moby-Dick* in 1851. This is his most famous book, but it was not successful at that time. In 1856 he wrote his most famous short stories, *Benito Cereno* and *Bartleby the Scrivener*. He also wrote books of poems.

He could not make enough money from his writing, so he took a government job. He held this job until 1885.

Billy Budd, Sailor

HERMAN MELVILLE

Level 3

Retold by Mary Gladwin
Series Editors: Andy Hopkins and Jocelyn Potter

Pearson Education Limited
Edinburgh Gate, Harlow,
Essex CM20 2JE, England
and Associated Companies throughout the world.

ISBN 0 582 34299 6

First published by University of Chicago Press 1962
This edition first published 2000

Typeset by Ferdinand Pageworks, London
Set in 11/14pt Bembo
Printed in Spain by Mateu Cromo, S. A. Pinto (Madrid)

Published by Pearson Education Limited in association with
Penguin Books Ltd, both companies being subsidiaries of Pearson Plc

For a complete list of the titles available in the Penguin Readers series please write to your local
Pearson Education office or to: Marketing Department, Penguin Longman Publishing,
5 Bentinck Street, London W1M 5RN.

Contents

Herman Melville died in New York in 1891, a short time after he wrote *Billy Budd, Sailor.*

Billy Budd, Sailor is the story of a young sailor, and it happens on a warship more than 200 years ago. But people everywhere still ask themselves the same questions today. What is right and what is wrong? And who can judge? Every reader can find their own answers in the story of Billy Budd.

The Bellipotent, *1797*

Chapter 1   The Handsome Sailor

At the time of the sailing ships, there were always groups of sailors in the big cities on the coast. They arrived on the warships and the merchant ships, and they walked through the streets in their best clothes.

There was often one man who was different from the other sailors in the group. He walked in the center like a king, with the other men around him like bodyguards. We can call him the Handsome Sailor.

I saw a man like that in Liverpool, fifty years ago. He was a very tall African, with a long piece of bright cloth around his neck. He wore big gold earrings and a colorful hat. He was walking in the middle of a group of sailors from every nation. They were laughing and joking together.

The people in the street stopped and looked at him in surprise. The sailors smiled back at them, proudly walking with their handsome friend.

At that time, the Handsome Sailor was good at his work, and he was also a good fighter. Many stories were told about his adventures. On land, he fought for his friends, and on the ship he was the bravest sailor and the hardest worker. The Handsome Sailor was popular with ordinary men because he usually had a good heart, too.

Billy Budd looked like a Handsome Sailor, but he wasn't exactly like the others. In 1797, he was twenty-one years old, and he was a sailor in the British Navy. Just before this story begins, he was working on a merchant ship, the *Rights-of-Man*. It was returning home to England and was near the coast.

At the same time, a British warship was leaving for the Mediterranean. Its name was the HMS *Bellipotent*. There weren't enough men on this ship, so the captain sent an officer to the *Rights-of-Man*.

In those days, when the captain of a warship needed men, he forced them into the Navy. He took them from the cities or from other ships, and so they became sailors in the service of the King.

So, Lieutenant Ratcliffe came from the *Bellipotent* to look at the sailors on the merchant ship. He chose Billy Budd, immediately. He didn't take any of the other men, and he didn't give a reason. Maybe the other men weren't as big and strong as Billy. Maybe he saw that there weren't many sailors on the *Rights-of-Man*.

Billy didn't look unhappy when he was chosen. Lieutenant Ratcliffe was pleased, but the other sailors were surprised. The captain of the merchant ship was also surprised, and he looked unhappily at the young sailor.

Captain Graveling was a good man, around fifty years old. He was heavy, with a round, intelligent face. His chosen job was a difficult one, but he also liked a quiet life. On a fine day, with a good wind, he was calm and his voice was musical. He was very careful, and he did his job well. Sometimes, though, he worried a lot. When his ship was near land, Captain Graveling couldn't sleep. He was more serious about his work than many other captains.

While Billy was packing his clothes, the *Bellipotent*'s lieutenant went to the captain's cabin. The captain didn't invite him to come in because he was thinking about other things. That didn't stop the lieutenant. He invited himself into the cabin, opened a cupboard, and took out a bottle. The lieutenant always did his work correctly, but he often seemed to need a strong drink.

The captain silently placed a glass and some water in front of his uninvited guest. The captain didn't want to drink with the lieutenant. He watched unhappily while the other man poured a small amount of water into his drink. The lieutenant emptied the glass quickly, then put it down, but not too far away from him. He sat comfortably in his chair and looked at the captain.

The captain looked back at him sadly and broke the silence. "Lieutenant, you're going to take my best man away from me," he said.

"Yes, I know," replied the other man. "Sorry." He filled his glass again.

"Excuse me, but you don't understand, Lieutenant," said the captain. "Before that young man came onto my ship, the men were always fighting. Life was terrible in those days, and I was worried all the time. I didn't even enjoy smoking my pipe. Then Billy arrived, and the men became calm. He didn't say anything, and he didn't do anything. He was just good, and his goodness changed the others. They loved him like flies love sugar.

"There was only one man who didn't like him. His name was Redbeard. I don't know why he didn't like Billy. Billy was always friendly with everyone. This man probably thought that he was weak. He wanted to fight with Billy, but Billy was always nice to him. He's like me, Lieutenant. He hates fighting.

"But one day, Redbeard and the other men were talking together and joking. Redbeard laughed and said, 'Look! If you want a steak, you cut it there!' He worked in a meat store before he joined the Navy. Then he pushed his finger hard into Billy's side.

"Billy didn't stop and think. He hit Redbeard hard, and he knocked him down. Billy didn't want to hurt him. I'm sure of that. The fight was finished in less than half a minute. Redbeard was very surprised. But now, he loves Billy Budd. He really loves him. But they all love him. They wash his clothes and they repair his old pants for him. They'll do anything for Billy Budd, and they're a happy family.

"But Lieutenant, if that young man leaves, there'll be trouble on the *Rights*. I know that. I won't be able to smoke my pipe quietly after dinner. Billy keeps the others calm, and now you're going to take him away." The poor captain was almost crying.

The lieutenant was still drinking happily. He was amused when he heard this. "So this young man is calm, but he can fight. Is that right?" He pointed out the cabin window. "He's like the seventy-four cannon on that warship there. They're calm, but they can fight, too."

He took another drink. "Be brave, man!" he said to the captain. "The King will be pleased when he hears about this. He needs a lot of sailors, but few men want to join the Navy. And some captains are angry when we borrow a few sailors for the King's service. But you're giving me your best man without any trouble. And this sailor didn't say a word when we chose him. Yes, the King will be very happy."

He stood up and looked out the cabin door. "But where's my handsome young man? Ah, there he is," he said. Billy was carrying a big box. The lieutenant stepped outside the cabin. "You can't take that onto a warship, boy," he said to Billy. "Put your clothes into a bag."

Billy and the lieutenant got into a small boat with some sailors from the warship. As the boat moved away from the *Rights-of-Man*, the officers and the sailors could read its name. Some of the men were amused.

"Look at that!" said one man. "The men on that ship have rights. But what about us? What are our rights?"

Nobody answered, and some of the others looked angrily at the ship's name. Then Billy jumped to his feet. He waved his hat at his friends as they watched him sadly from the merchant ship. "Goodbye, boys!" he called. He waved his hat again. "And goodbye to you, too, old *Rights-of-Man*!"

"Sit down, sir!" shouted the lieutenant, hiding a smile. "You can't do that in the Navy!" Of course, Billy didn't know that. But the lieutenant was shouting at him for another reason.

"And goodbye to you, too, old Rights-of-Man*!"*

"He was laughing at the Navy and at me!" he thought. "He was forced into the Navy. He didn't choose to join it. So he was saying goodbye to his rights as a man."

But Billy didn't think like that. He was a simple and honest young man, and he was only saying goodbye to his friends.

Chapter 2   Billy Budd

When Billy was taken into the Navy, he obeyed immediately. He accepted this change as he accepted changes in the weather. Or maybe he wasn't unhappy about it, and he was hoping for an adventure.

He was soon at home on the *Bellipotent*. The other sailors liked him because he was good-looking and happy. He was very different from the other men. They were often sad or angry when they weren't working. Some of them had homes and families, and they worried about them. But Billy was younger than the other men, and he didn't have a family.

On the merchant ships, Billy was always very popular. Everybody knew him and liked him. Life was different for him when he left the *Rights-of-Man* for the great warship. Some of the men on the *Bellipotent* were friendly, but others didn't notice him. The older men knew more than he did about the Navy and about the world.

Billy was like a pretty young girl who comes from the country to the palace of the King. She is compared with all the beautiful ladies there. But Billy didn't compare himself with the others. He didn't notice when some of the hard-faced sailors smiled strangely at him. And he didn't see the smiles of some of the officers.

Their interest in Billy wasn't surprising. He was young, and he looked younger than his age. He had a man's body, but his face was more like a woman's. His skin was brown from the sun, but his face was pink. His face was strong, but his nose and mouth were small and well-shaped. His hands were rough, but fine. He didn't look like a sailor, and he didn't move like one. He looked like a rich man's son.

This was a mystery until one of the officers asked Billy some questions.

"Where were you born?" he asked.

"I don't know, sir," replied Billy.

"You don't know?" continued the officer. "Who was your father?"

"I don't know, sir."

The officer was surprised. "Do you know anything about your birth?"

"No, sir. But I've heard that I was found in Bristol. Someone left me outside a rich man's door. I was dressed in pretty clothes."

"You were found?" said the officer, looking carefully at Billy. "I hope we can find some more men like you. We need them in the Navy!"

Yes, everyone could see that Billy came from a good family. We can always see when a racehorse has good blood.

Billy was healthy and intelligent, but he couldn't read or write. He was a good singer, and sometimes he sang his own songs. He was handsome, but he wasn't too proud. He didn't think about it.

He liked to be outdoors. He knew a lot about the sea, but he didn't know much about the land. Like most sailors, he only knew the coast. Sailors stay near the sea when they leave their ships. They can always find dance-houses, women, and drinking-houses there. Billy went to these places. He didn't think it was wrong. All the sailors went there, and those men weren't good or bad. They were on the ship for a long time, and they worked hard. Then they went onto the land to enjoy themselves. They weren't as bad as the men who live on land. Those men are often dishonest and mean.

Billy wasn't like that. He was simple and good. But he had a problem that nobody could see. When his ship was in danger from bad weather, he was an excellent sailor. But when he suddenly had strong feelings in his heart, he stuttered. When he was calm, his voice was musical. But when he was excited, the words didn't always come.

Now we know that the Handsome Sailor wasn't perfect. And this also tells us that his story is not a happy one.

Chapter 3   Captain Vere

After Billy came onto the *Bellipotent*, the ship joined other English ships in the Mediterranean. Sometimes, the *Bellipotent* sailed alone and looked for enemy ships. It was faster than the others. Other times, they all stayed together.

It was the summer of 1797. In April of that year, there was a serious mutiny at Spithead. Then the Great Mutiny followed in May. The lives of sailors on the ships were very hard, and thousands of them refused to obey their officers' orders. The Navy punished many of these men. But they also listened to them, so the mutinies ended.

Some things got better, but there were still problems. Before the mutinies, some companies were selling bad food and poor cloth to the Navy. The Navy stopped that, but they still forced men onto their sailing ships. Each ship had many sails and cannon, and there were thousands of ships. They always needed more men. And the Navy was building more ships to protect England against its European enemies.

Many of the men were still unhappy after the Two Mutinies. The ships' captains watched them carefully for signs of trouble. The officers watched them when they fired the cannon at enemy ships. Sometimes, the officers stood behind them with their guns in their hands.

But the officers and the men of the *Bellipotent* were calm, even a short time after the Great Mutiny. On a warship, the officers act like the captain, if he is a strong man.

Captain Edward Fairfax Vere was an excellent sailor, at a time when there were many famous seamen. He was around forty, he wasn't married, and he came from a good family, but this didn't help him become a captain. He was in the Navy for years, and he fought many times against the enemy's ships. After the English won against the French in the West Indies, he was made a captain.

Captain Vere's men were important to him, and he wanted them to be happy. But they had to obey him. He was a brave man, but never careless.

On land, nobody knew that he was in the Navy. He wore ordinary clothes, and he didn't use naval language.

At sea, his face was serious, except when he went into action. Sometimes he stood alone on the deck of the ship, looking out over the water. At these times, he had a dreamy look on his face. When someone spoke to him, he looked quite angry, but only for a second. He always became calm again very quickly.

In the Navy, they called him "Starry Vere." One of his cousins gave him this name. He found it in a poem about a brave soldier called Vere. When Captain Vere returned from the West Indies, his cousin came to meet him. "Good work, Ed, my starry Vere," he said. He was proud that there was a new captain in the family. The name stayed with Captain Vere, and everyone used it. There was another Captain Vere in the Navy at that time, so it was useful.

Captain Vere was an excellent naval officer, and he was also an unusual man. He was intelligent, and he was interested in many things, not only life at sea. He always added new books to his library before his ship sailed. He had some free time away from land, but he was never bored.

Captain Edward Fairfax Vere

He wasn't interested in literature. He enjoyed reading about history and the lives of great men. He also liked to read about science and religion. His books helped him form strong opinions. The world was changing around him, but he always knew his own mind.

He was very different from the other officers. "He isn't very friendly," they thought. "He's only interested in his books." Sometimes they talked about him, too. "Vere is a fine man," they said. "He's a good seaman and a good fighter. But don't you think he's strange? He's not like a Navy man. He's like a guest of the King on this ship."

The other officers were right when they said this. He never joked with the other men, and he didn't use ordinary language. When they talked about the day's news, he talked about the history of the world. When they talked about famous people, he talked about dead kings or naval officers. The other officers didn't read the same books, so they didn't understand him. But Captain Vere didn't realize this, so his conversation didn't change.

Chapter 4   John Claggart

John Claggart was the officer of the guard. His job was to keep order on the gun decks. He was like a police chief on the ship. He was a tall, thin man of around thirty-five. He had small, fine hands; thick, black hair; and an intelligent face. His skin was very pale because he never went out in the sun. He looked almost unhealthy next to the red and brown faces of the sailors.

The officer of the guard looked like a man from a good family, but nobody knew anything about him. Was he English? Or was he French? Did he learn the language when he was a child? Was he in trouble with the law? Nobody knew. They knew that many sailors joined the Navy for this reason. And when the Navy needed more men, they sometimes took them from the prisons.

Claggart was an adult when he joined the Navy. He started at the bottom, and he worked hard. He was serious, always obeyed orders, and soon became the officer of the guard. The men knew this, but they knew nothing about his life on land. Of course, a ship's chief of police is never popular with the sailors, so the men often made up stories about his past.

Claggart chose a number of ship's corporals to help him with his work. They watched and listened to the other sailors and reported this information back to the officer of the guard. His spies were everywhere on the ship.

Billy Budd was quite happy on the *Bellipotent*. He worked high up on the topsails, at the front of the ship. He and the other young men were topmen because they were good climbers. When they weren't busy, they sat up there. They talked, and watched the others on the decks far below.

Billy was a good worker, and he was always ready to help. He was like that when he was on the merchant ship, too. Sometimes his friends laughed at him because of this. "Why do you obey orders so quickly?" they asked him.

There was a reason—he was afraid. One day, a young sailor was away from his place when the ship was turning around. Nobody tied down his sail, and the ship was in difficulty. The sailor was punished for this in front of all the others. Another man hit him again and again on his back until it was red with blood. Billy saw the terrible look of pain on the man's face. "I'll always do my work well," he promised himself. "I don't want that to happen to me!"

But Billy did have some trouble with the ship's corporals.

"Put away your clothes!" said one.

"Don't leave your bag there!" said another.

Billy was worried, and he spoke to the other topmen about the corporals. "I can't understand it," he said. "Why are they always watching me? And why do they talk to me like that? I always try to do everything right." His friends only laughed at him.

Billy remembered a wise old Danish sailor that he knew. "I'll talk to him," he thought. "Maybe he can help me." The old man's long years on the ocean showed on his sunburned face. Under one eye, there was an old cut from an attack on an enemy ship. There were little pieces of blue metal in his skin from an accident on the gun deck. They called him "Old Blue Smoke" because of this.

The first time he saw Billy Budd, he smiled quietly to himself. He was probably surprised to see a Handsome Sailor on a warship. Maybe he asked himself, "What will happen to that boy? He's young and innocent and he doesn't know anything."

But the old Dane liked Billy when he knew him better. Billy always spoke politely to him as they passed on the ship. Old people always like that. And the old man gave Billy the name that everyone called him, "Baby Budd." Maybe it was a joke. Maybe it was because Billy was much younger than him. Or maybe there was another reason.

Billy went to see the old Dane about his problem with the ship's corporals. The Dane was sitting on a box, watching the other sailors. He listened carefully to Billy, and there was a strange light in his little dark eyes.

When he finished his story, Billy said, "Tell me what you think. Please."

The old sailor touched the cut on his face and thought for a minute. "Baby Budd," he said quietly, "Longlegs is against you."

Billy's blue eyes became big and round. "Claggart! The officer of the guard?" he asked in a surprised voice. "He can't be against me! He calls me 'that nice, sweet young man.' The others told me that."

"Is that right?" asked the old sailor. He smiled again. "Yes, it's possible," he said. "I know that Longlegs has a sweet voice."

"He doesn't always have a sweet voice," replied Billy. "But he always speaks nicely to me when I pass him."

"Because he's against you!"

"And why?" asked Old Blue Smoke. "Because he's against you!"

Billy was even more worried now. "Why am I in trouble with the corporals?" he asked himself. "And is Longlegs really against me? Why? I don't understand anything!"

He looked at the old seaman. "What do you mean? Please explain it to me," he said.

But the wise old seaman refused to say another word.

Chapter 5   An Angry Man

Billy didn't believe the old sailor's story when he heard it. And he didn't believe it the next day, when Claggart spoke to him again.

Billy and his friends were talking and laughing and eating lunch together. Then the ship moved suddenly, and Billy's soup bowl fell from the table. There was soup everywhere on the clean deck.

The officer of the guard walked past, carrying a stick. He prepared to be very angry as he stepped over the soup. But then he noticed Billy, and he stopped himself.

He looked at Billy and pointed down at the soup. "That's very handsome," he said with a little smile. His voice was low and musical. He hit Billy lightly on the back with his stick. "And you're very handsome, too!" He turned his back and walked away.

Billy and his friends didn't see the angry smile on Claggart's face as he spoke. "He's making a joke," they thought. They all laughed loudly because he was an officer. And Billy laughed because the officer called him a "Handsome Sailor." He turned to his friends and said, "You see, Longlegs isn't against me!"

Another sailor, Donald, looked at him in surprise. "Who says that he's against you, Beautiful?" he asked.

Billy didn't reply. He thought about the old Dane. "Only one

Claggart continued along the path.

other person thinks that Longlegs is against me," he said to himself. "Maybe I was wrong."

Claggart continued along the path. Nobody could see him now, so he didn't hide his angry look. Then suddenly, a young sailor ran around a corner and surprised him. His shoulder touched Claggart's lightly as they met. "Be careful!" shouted the officer. He gave him a sharp cut with his stick. The young sailor looked at him strangely and walked quickly away.

So what *was* the matter with Claggart? And why was he angry with Billy Budd? He never spoke to him on the ship. Billy was always calm, and he kept the others calm. And in Claggart's words, he was a "nice, sweet young man." So why was Claggart against Billy? This was a mystery.

Did the officer know Billy before he saw him on the warship? No. Did he dislike the young sailor because he was very different from him? No. When many different types of men live together on a warship, they can't make enemies.

In this world, some men are good and others are bad. Some men are born bad, and they never change. Some go to prison, and some are hanged for their crimes. Others are more intelligent and more careful. They don't drink wine, they don't steal, and they don't make enemies.

Everyone thinks that these men are good. Their minds are calm, and they are very smart. But their hearts are angry. These men are the most dangerous of all the bad, mad men.

Why? Because they aren't mad all of the time. They become mad only when they are near a special somebody or something. And it is a secret madness that nobody can see. They look like ordinary men.

Claggart was one of these men. Some men become bad, and mad, while they are growing up. Others learn about madness from books. And some become mad because they live bad lives with bad people. But Claggart was already mad when he was born.

Claggart was very different from Billy. We have already seen that. Claggart was tall and pale, but Billy was strong and handsome. Claggart had an intelligent face. Billy didn't look intelligent, but he had a good heart. This showed on his face. The officer of the guard always dressed carefully, but he wasn't handsome. Was he against Billy for that reason? What did he mean when he called Billy handsome? His voice was angry when he said it. But the other sailors didn't hear that.

Billy was a healthy young man, and he enjoyed life. Claggart hated him for that. But he hated Billy Budd for another reason. Billy's heart was simple and good, and he never hurt anybody. He had the body and the mind of a Handsome Sailor.

Yes, Claggart hated Billy because he was handsome. But he also wanted to be like Billy. His feelings about Billy—for Billy?—were strong. They came from the heart and not from the mind. Nobody ever talks about these feelings. They keep them secret. But the feelings don't go away.

Billy was perfectly innocent, and only Claggart really knew that. When he realized it, he hated Billy more and more. Because Claggart was the opposite of Billy—he was completely bad. He couldn't change that, but he could hide it from other people. He turned his feelings of hate against himself and against Billy.

Everybody, rich and poor, can have strong feelings. And sometimes, a little thing makes a person very angry. This can happen anywhere. In this story, it happened on a clean deck on a warship, and the little thing was a sailor's bowl of soup.

The officer of the guard saw the bowl of soup when it fell onto the deck in front of him. It was Billy's soup, and he knew that. It wasn't an accident. He was sure of that, too. "Billy Budd hates me because I hate him," he thought. "But I'm much stronger than him."

After that, one of his corporals told him stories about Billy, and Claggart believed him. The other sailors called the corporal

"Sharp" because he spied on them with his sharp eyes and his sharp ears.

Claggart asked this man to watch Billy, and Sharp quickly understood. "Claggart doesn't like him," he said to himself. He followed the young sailor and watched and listened to him.

Sharp reported everything to Claggart. When Billy was having fun with his friends, he told the officer of the guard. And he said things that weren't true. "He calls you names," he told his chief. "He calls you 'Longlegs', and he laughs at you."

Claggart believed all these stories. The men didn't like him and he knew that. The sailors on a warship never like the officer of the guard, and they always laugh at him. But Claggart wanted to believe Sharp's stories. He wanted a good reason to hate Billy.

"Billy dropped the soup on purpose," thought Claggart. "He calls me names behind my back." These stories were little things, but they made him very angry. Was Claggart sorry about these feelings? No. "I'm right and Billy Budd is wrong," he thought. And Sharp helped him prove it.

Chapter 6   A Strange Meeting

A few days later, something strange happened to Billy. It was a warm night, and Billy went to sleep on the lower gun deck. But he was too hot, so he went up to a higher deck for air. He lay down below the topsails where he worked during the day. He had permission to sleep there because he worked there. Three other men from the lower deck were already sleeping there.

He woke up slowly when somebody touched his shoulder. A voice spoke urgently in his ear. "Billy! Go to the outside deck! Don't speak! Something's happening! Quick! I'll meet you there!"

Billy was a kind young man, and he didn't like to say "no" to people. And he wanted to know what was happening. He wasn't afraid to go. He was still sleepy, so he didn't think about it. For all these reasons, he went to meet the other sailor.

The sailor soon joined Billy Budd on a narrow deck that hung over the sea. Nobody could see them. There was no moon, and clouds hid the stars. Billy couldn't see the man's face clearly. "I think I've seen him before," he thought. "I think he's one of the watchmen from the back deck." Billy's guess was right.

"Billy!" the man said. "You were forced onto this ship, weren't you?" He spoke in the same quick, quiet voice. Billy didn't answer. He didn't know what to say. The man continued. "There's a big gang of men like us on this ship, Billy. We aren't the only ones. You'll help us, won't you?"

Billy was awake now. "What do you mean?" he asked loudly.

"Be quiet!" said the voice quickly. "Look!" The man held two small, round shiny things in his hand. "You can have them if you'll . . ."

Billy stopped him. He spoke quickly, so he began to stutter. "I d-d-don't know what you w-w-want. Now g-g-go away!" The man was surprised. When he didn't move, Billy jumped to his feet. "G-go away," he shouted, "or I'll th-th-throw you into the water!" The other man finally understood the message and quickly disappeared into the shadows.

Billy's voice woke up one of the other sailors. "What's the matter?" he called. Then he saw Billy. "Ah, Beautiful, it's you," he said. "What's wrong? I heard you stutter."

Billy wasn't stuttering now. "I saw a watchman from the back deck," he replied quickly. "I found him here, in our part of the ship. So I told him to go away."

"Why didn't you keep him here, Topman?" asked another voice angrily. It was an old sailor with red hair and a red face. "If we catch a spy here, we'll punish him!"

The other sailors believed Billy's story. They were topmen, and they worked on the top decks and with the high topsails. They

"G-go away or I'll th-th-throw you into the water!"

didn't like the men from the back decks. "They're like men who live on land," they said. "They never climb up high and they aren't good sailors."

The next day, Billy thought about his strange meeting. He didn't understand. "Why did that watchman come to see me?" he asked himself. Billy didn't know him. The watchman worked on a lower deck at the back of the ship, and Billy worked on the top deck at the front.

"What did he want?" he thought. "And what was he holding in his hand? Was it money? They looked like gold pieces. Where did they come from?" Billy couldn't find the answers to these questions. He didn't want to ask the watchman. "I'm sure that he's bad," he thought. "But I'd like to see him in the daylight."

The next morning, Billy saw a man who looked like the watchman. He was with a group of men who were smoking on the top gun deck. But he wasn't sure. "Is that him?" he asked himself. "He's the same size and shape as the man I saw last night. But I didn't see his face."

The watchman was short and heavy, and he was about Billy's age. He had a round face and light blue eyes. He was talking and laughing with the other sailors. The man noticed Billy before Billy saw him. When Billy looked at him, he smiled in a friendly way. "He doesn't look like a man who's planning a mutiny," thought Billy.

A day or two later, the man said "hello" to Billy as he passed him on a gun deck. Billy was surprised and nervous, so he didn't reply.

Billy was more worried now. He didn't understand what was happening. He didn't report the strange meeting to an officer. He didn't think of that. Also, he didn't like to tell stories about the other men.

At first, he didn't tell anybody. Then, after a few days, he spoke to the old Danish sailor. It was a calm night, and they were sitting together on deck. Billy didn't tell him everything, but Old Blue Smoke guessed the rest.

"Baby Budd, I was right, wasn't I?" he said.

"What do you mean?" asked Billy.

"Longlegs is against you."

"Longlegs?" repeated Billy in surprise. "I was talking about that crazy watchman, not about Longlegs!"

"Oh, is he a watchman? You didn't tell me that, did you?" said the old man. "Now I understand. Somebody sent him to see you." He slowly lit his pipe and smoked it silently.

Billy was full of questions. "Who? Why? What do you mean?"

But Old Blue Smoke didn't say anything. After his long years in the Navy, he knew when he should be quiet.

"Am I in trouble because of the officer of the guard?" Billy asked himself. "It can't be true! Longlegs always speaks kindly to me."

Billy didn't believe it because he was as innocent as a child. Children become more intelligent when they grow up. They are not as innocent when they become adults. But when Billy grew up, he stayed innocent. Also, he didn't know very much about life. He only knew about ships and sailors.

Sailors are different from the men who live on land. Most seamen are honest and simple; landmen are often dishonest. Many sailors never grow up. They obey orders and they don't ask any questions.

On land, the rules aren't the same. Every man makes his own rules. And every man has to be careful of the others. They can hurt him or trick him. Everyone on land knows that, but the sailors don't.

Billy didn't have anymore trouble after his accident with the bowl of soup. Nobody told him to put away his clothes or his bag. And the officer of the guard's smiles and kind words were friendly.

But Claggart wasn't always smiling. Sometimes, he watched Billy walking along the gun deck with his friends. They were laughing and joking. When nobody was watching him, he followed Billy with sad eyes. At other times, he had a soft look in his eyes. Maybe it was a look of love. And maybe he was sad because this love was impossible. It couldn't be.

But these looks quickly disappeared, and his eyes were cold again. If he saw Billy coming, he smiled at him kindly. But when he met him suddenly, an angry red light shone from his eyes.

Billy saw some of these looks, but he didn't understand them. "Longlegs acts very strangely sometimes," he thought. "But I think he likes me. He always speaks kindly to me." Billy was as innocent as a child. He did his work well and he didn't do anything wrong. So he wasn't afraid of Claggart.

And he wasn't worried when two officers looked at him in a strangely unfriendly way. This happened more than once. Billy didn't know them because he didn't work for them. Did somebody say something to them about Billy? These officers ate at the same table as the officer of the guard, and they often talked together. Billy knew this, but he didn't think about it. And he wasn't worried about the two officers because he was popular with the other men.

Billy didn't see the watchman very often because they didn't work together. He spoke to Billy when he passed. But they never discussed their first meeting.

But why didn't Billy talk to him about that night? Why didn't he talk to some of the other men who were forced onto the ship? Were those men unhappy? Were they planning a mutiny? We don't know. Billy was simple and innocent, so he didn't ask any questions.

And Claggart continued to watch Billy. He thought about him all the time. He looked calm on the outside, but he was burning inside.

Chapter 7   Trouble

Nothing important happened for some time after Billy's strange meeting with the watchman.

We have already seen that the *Bellipotent* was a very good sailing ship. It was fast and it could turn quickly. It also had an excellent captain. For these reasons, it sometimes sailed away alone to look for enemy ships.

One afternoon, the *Bellipotent* met a French warship when it was far from the other ships. The enemy had more men and more guns than Captain Vere's ship. So, he gave the order to turn around, and they sailed quickly back toward the other English ships. The men worked hard for hours, but the other ship followed close behind. The *Bellipotent* finally escaped after dark when the French ship turned back.

Soon after this, the officer of the guard went to see Captain Vere. The captain was walking around the outside deck, still thinking about the enemy ship. Claggart stood waiting with his hat in his hand. Finally, the captain turned and noticed him.

Captain Vere was surprised to see him. Officers like Claggart didn't usually speak to the captain. And he didn't know Claggart very well because he was new. Claggart took the place of another officer of the guard just before Billy Budd arrived on the ship.

Captain Vere gave Claggart a strange look. He didn't know him, but already he didn't like him. "What do you want?" he said impatiently.

"I'm sorry, sir," said Claggart. "There's a problem. I saw something earlier today when we were sailing away from the other ships. There's a dangerous man on this ship. He didn't want to join the Navy. And he isn't the only one. I saw him talking to the others. There's a gang of them."

"What do you mean?" asked the captain. "Are you talking about the men who didn't choose to join this ship?"

"Yes, sir," continued Claggart. "I didn't want to say anything. I wasn't sure before, but now I know. They're planning something."

Captain Vere was worried. But was the man's story true? He continued to listen to the officer.

"I'm sure that you don't want a mutiny on the *Bellipotent*," Claggart finished.

"Be quiet!" said the captain angrily. His officers never spoke to him like that. And they never used the word "mutiny." "Is he trying to worry me?" the captain asked himself. "Why? What does he want?" Captain Vere didn't want to believe Claggart. He wanted him to prove his story.

"You say there's a dangerous man. Tell me his name," he said.

Claggart's answer was ready. "William Budd, a topman, sir."

"William Budd!" repeated the captain in surprise. "Is he the man that Lieutenant Ratcliffe brought from the merchant ship? Is he the man who's so popular? Do they call him 'Billy, the Handsome Sailor'?"

"Yes, sir. That's the man," replied Claggart. "He's young and good-looking, but he's dangerous. He's friendly with the others, so they'll say nice things about him. And you know what he said on Lieutenant Ratcliffe's boat: 'Goodbye to you, old *Rights-of-Man!*' Yes, he's always smiling, but he hides his feelings. He's unhappy because he never wanted to join the Navy. He looks handsome, but he's very dangerous."

The captain thought for a minute before he answered. "Billy Budd! I know who he is. And I remember his words when he joined us. I was pleased because Billy accepted his new job so easily. And I've always had good reports of Billy's work. I even wanted to give him a better job."

He thought about Claggart's last words. "Is Billy Budd really dangerous?" he asked himself. "We've never had any trouble on my ship."

"He's young and good-looking, but he's dangerous."

The captain gave Claggart a cold look. "Is your story true?" he asked. "Be careful. If you're lying, I'll have to punish you."

Claggart shook his head sadly. "I'm sorry, sir, it's true," he said. "And I can prove it."

Captain Vere looked into Claggart's eyes, then turned away. "Can he prove it?" he asked himself. "What can I do?" He decided to talk to Billy Budd.

He wanted to do this quietly. He didn't want the other men on the ship to know about this problem. The other officers were watching him as he talked to Claggart.

He turned to Claggart. "Is Budd working now?"

"No, sir," replied the officer of the guard.

The captain called one of the officers. "Mr. Wilkes, tell Albert to come here."

Albert was his cabin boy. "Do you know Budd, the topman?" he asked.

"Yes, sir," replied the boy.

"Go and find him," ordered the captain. "He isn't working now. Tell him to come with you. And speak quietly. I don't want the others to hear you. Then bring him to my cabin."

He turned to Claggart. "Wait on the deck below. Then, when Albert arrives with Budd, follow them."

Chapter 8   The Lie

Albert took Billy to the captain's cabin. Billy was surprised, but he wasn't worried. "I think the captain likes me," he thought. "Maybe he wants to give me a better job. Maybe he'll ask the officer of the guard about me." He didn't feel the danger that was all around him.

"Shut the door, guard," said the captain. "Don't let anybody in here."

"Now, Claggart," he said. "Tell this man what you told me."

Claggart moved close to Billy. He looked deep into his eyes as he repeated his story.

At first, Billy didn't understand. Then his face turned pale and his blue eyes opened wide. Claggart's eyes were burning. Billy listened without moving. He couldn't say a word.

Captain Vere was watching the two men. "Speak, man!" he said to Billy. "Defend yourself!"

Billy tried to obey. He shook his head and waved his arms, and strange noises came from his mouth. He tried to speak with his body, but he couldn't. There was surprise and fear in his eyes.

Captain Vere didn't know about Billy's problem, but he soon understood. He moved closer to the young sailor and put a hand on his shoulder. "Speak slowly, my boy," he said kindly. "Don't hurry."

These words touched Billy's heart. He tried harder to speak, but he couldn't. There was pain in his eyes.

Suddenly, his right arm moved as quickly as a shot from a cannon, and Claggart fell to the floor. Did Billy know what he was doing? Or did it only happen because he was taller than Claggart? Billy hit the officer of the guard just above his eyes. The officer's body fell back and lay without moving.

"Are you mad, boy? What have you done?" cried the captain. "Help me!"

They tried to pull Claggart up into a sitting position, but he was heavy and they couldn't move him. They lowered the body back onto the floor.

Captain Vere stood up and covered his face with his hands. He stood quietly for a minute, thinking.

When he slowly uncovered his face, he looked like a captain again, not the kind father of a few minutes earlier. And he spoke like a naval officer, too.

"Go in there!" he said to Billy. He pointed to a small

Suddenly, his right arm moved.

room. "And stay there until I call you!" Billy obeyed silently.

The captain opened the outside door and called Albert. "Tell the doctor to come here," he ordered. "And don't come back until I call you."

The doctor came to the cabin. "Look at this man," said Vere.

The doctor looked at Claggart in surprise. His face was white, and thick, black blood was slowly running from his ear and his nose. The man was dead. The doctor knew that immediately.

The captain wanted to be sure. "*Is* he dead?" he asked. "Look at him carefully, and then tell me."

The doctor obeyed, but he also looked strangely at the captain. The captain didn't see him; he was standing with his hand over his eyes. Suddenly, he took the doctor's arm. "Look!" he said excitedly, pointing at the body. "He told a lie and he was punished for it!"

The doctor was surprised again, but he didn't speak. "Why is there a dead man in the captain's cabin?" he asked himself. "Why hasn't he explained it to me?"

The captain continued. "He was punished. But we know who punished him! And that man has to die!" His voice became calmer, and he told the story to the doctor.

"Help me move him," he said to the doctor. He pointed to a small room opposite the room where Billy was waiting.

The doctor obeyed again, but he was worried. "Why is he keeping this secret?" he asked himself. "Why doesn't he want anybody to know?"

But the captain was calm now. "Go," he said to the doctor. "I shall call a court soon. Tell the lieutenants what has happened. And tell them not to talk about it to anybody."

The doctor was more worried now. "Is the captain mad?" he asked himself. "Or is he just excited after Claggart's death? And why is he calling a court? I don't think that's a good idea. The captain should keep Billy in the ship's prison until we return to land. Is Vere mad? I can't prove it. What can I do? I can't question the captain's orders. And if I disobey them, that is mutiny."

So, the doctor told the lieutenants about Claggart's death. He didn't say anything about the captain's excitement.

The other officers agreed with the doctor about the court. They were surprised and worried, too.

"We should wait," said the first lieutenant. "We should have the court on land, not here at sea."

Chapter 9   A Secret Meeting

When is a man mad? What is the difference between a healthy mind and an unhealthy one? How do we know? When a man is truly mad, we know. It is more difficult when somebody is only a little mad. Only a doctor can tell us that.

"The captain *is* mad!" thought the ship's doctor. "I know when it happened. It was very sudden. It was when Billy killed the officer of the guard."

We, of course, can decide for ourselves. We know that Claggart's death happened at a very bad time. It was just after the mutinies. All the ships' captains were watching their men carefully. All crimes were quickly punished.

But this crime was unusual. The officer of the guard told a lie about an innocent man. He was guilty of lying. But the innocent man was also guilty. He killed the man who lied. So, he was a criminal. He killed an officer, and in the Navy this was a very serious crime. It was the same as mutiny. The captain knew that Billy was a good man. He knew that Claggart was not. But he had to obey the law.

The captain of the *Bellipotent* usually made quick decisions. But now he needed time to think. But he also wanted to keep Billy's crime secret, so he didn't wait long. This was probably a mistake.

Some of the other officers talked about it later. "Why didn't he wait?" they said. "He was wrong." Captain Vere's friends and family, of course, didn't agree.

"I'd like to wait," thought the captain, "but I can't. I must do my job. A sailor has killed an officer. Soon, the other men will know about it. When they hear the news, then a mutiny will start. I must stop it before it begins. And I must act quickly!"

Captain Vere chose three officers for the court: the first lieutenant, the sea lieutenant, and the sailing officer. "They'll decide if the topman is innocent or guilty," thought the captain. "I'll listen, and I'll watch. They can ask me questions if they need to. And then I'll decide what to do. I'm the captain, and I must decide."

The three officers were all very different, and they came from different parts of the ship.

"The first lieutenant is a kind, thoughtful man and a good seaman," the captain said to himself. "He enjoys the good things in life—eating and sleeping—and he's very smart. But will he make the right decision? The other two officers are good sailors and brave fighters, but they aren't known for their intelligence."

The court met in the captain's cabin. Captain Vere had three rooms. One room was now a prison, and Claggart's body lay in another. There was a long room between these two rooms, with two small, round windows at each end.

They brought the prisoner into the long room, and Captain Vere spoke first. He didn't speak because he was the captain. He spoke because he was there at the death of the officer of the guard. He told the court everything. He repeated Claggart's lie about Billy. And he described Billy's actions when he heard it.

The officers looked at Billy Budd in surprise. Mutiny? Murder? He didn't look like a troublemaker or a murderer.

The first lieutenant spoke to the prisoner. "Captain Vere has spoken. Are his words true?"

The young sailor replied in a clear voice. "Yes, Captain Vere's words are true, but the officer of the guard was lying. I have eaten the King's bread, and I am the King's man."

"I believe you," said the captain, speaking from his heart.

"Th-th-thank you, sir," stuttered Billy. There were tears in his eyes.

The first lieutenant continued. "Were you and the officer of the guard enemies?"

Billy still spoke with difficulty. "No, there were no bad feelings between us. I wasn't against him. I'm sorry that he's dead. I didn't want to kill him. He lied to me and he lied to the captain. I wasn't planning any trouble. I wanted to speak, but the words didn't come. Then I hit him because I couldn't speak."

Billy spoke honestly from his heart. Captain Vere believed Billy, and now the court understood the reason.

The first lieutenant spoke again. "Was there any trouble on the ship? Were the men planning anything?" He didn't use the word "mutiny."

Billy waited before he gave his answer. "He can't speak," thought the officers of the court. But Billy was thinking about his strange meeting with the watchman. He didn't want to talk to the officers about the other sailors.

When a sailor hears about trouble on a ship, he must tell the officers. They can punish him if he doesn't. But Billy didn't say anything at the time, and he didn't say anything to the court now. He also didn't believe that the men were planning a mutiny.

"No," Billy said clearly. "There wasn't any trouble on the ship."

"I didn't want to kill him."

Chapter 10   "We must obey the law"

The sea lieutenant spoke to Billy for the first time. He looked worried. "The officer of the guard lied, and there were no bad feelings between you? So why did he lie? I don't understand."

Billy didn't reply. The other men watched him. "Is he trying to hide his guilt?" they asked themselves. Billy tried to speak, but again the words didn't come. He looked at Captain Vere and his eyes asked for help.

Captain Vere stood up and faced the sea lieutenant. "That was a good question," he said. "We all want to know the answer, but we'll never know it." He pointed at Billy. "This man can't reply. Only the dead man knows the answer, but he can't tell us now."

The captain looked at each of the three officers and continued to speak. "So we don't know why the officer of the guard acted that way. But we know what happened after that. We know that this man hit the officer of the guard. And we know that the officer of the guard died. This court doesn't need any other information."

Did Billy understand this? We don't know, but he looked at Captain Vere again and his eyes silently asked for help.

The three officers understood the captain. "He has already decided," they thought. "He thinks the prisoner is guilty. What can we do?"

The first lieutenant spoke to the other three. "We need more information. Can't anybody on the ship tell us anything? This is a mystery."

"Yes, there is a mystery," agreed the captain. "But this court doesn't need to know the answer. And we can't know the answer because that man will never speak again." The captain pointed at the closed door of the room where Claggart lay. "We know what the prisoner did. That's enough."

The sea lieutenant listened sadly and said nothing. Captain Vere made a sign with his head to the first lieutenant. The court continued its work.

The first lieutenant turned to the prisoner. "Budd, if you want to say something, say it now."

The young sailor looked quickly again at Captain Vere. He didn't find any help there. "I have nothing more to say, sir," he replied to the officer.

A guard took Billy back into the second small room next to the courtroom. As the two men disappeared, the three officers moved in their seats. They could talk more freely because Billy wasn't there. But they didn't know what to say. Each man looked at the others. They had to judge the prisoner quickly. They knew that.

Captain Vere stood with his back toward the three officers. He looked out at the sea through one of the round windows. It was getting dark outside.

The courtroom was silent most of the time. Sometimes the officers spoke in low, serious voices, then it was quiet again. The captain walked up and down, listening.

Finally, he stopped and stood in front of the officers. He looked carefully into each man's face. "I know what I want to say to them," he thought. "But how can I say it? I want them to understand."

These men were good seamen and good officers, but they didn't think like the captain. The captain read and studied and thought about life. He was a good captain, but his men didn't always understand him.

Finally, this is what he said:

"Until now, I have not acted like the captain in this court. I have only told you what happened. But now you don't know what to do. You know the law, but you feel sorry for the prisoner. I understand, because I feel the same way. But I can't feel this way. Something unusual happened this time, and we know it. But that doesn't change the law. This is a naval court, and we must obey the law at all times.

"What are your feelings? Where do they come from? Think carefully. We know that the officer of the guard lied. But we also know that the prisoner killed him. That is a very serious crime. So must the prisoner die for his crime? We all feel that he is, in every other way, an innocent man. Am I right?"

The three officers gave a sign with their heads.

"You all say 'yes,' and I do, too," continued the captain. "I feel the same way, but we can't listen to our feelings. We are the King's men, and we must obey his laws. We aren't free. When there is a war, does anybody ask us to fight? No, they *order* us to fight. It doesn't matter if we *want* to fight.

"And now the court must decide, and it must also follow the law. We can't decide if we like the law. We must obey it.

"I know that this story touches your hearts. It touches mine, too. Our hearts are warm, but our minds must be cold. What happens in a court on land? Does the judge listen to a prisoner's wife or mother when she cries? No, he can't. Our hearts are like this woman—and we can't listen to her."

The captain gave the men a long, serious look. "You all have your own private thoughts and opinions," he said. "But we are naval officers. We can't think like ordinary men. Isn't the King's law more important than our opinions?"

The three men moved uncomfortably in their seats. They couldn't answer the captain's question.

The captain saw this, and continued. "Here are the facts. If a man hits an officer in wartime at sea, the punishment is death. And this time, the officer died. And . . ."

"Yes, sir," the first lieutenant said, with tears in his eyes. "But Budd didn't want to kill him. And he wasn't planning a mutiny!"

"We know that, my good man," said the captain. "But we can't use that information. Other courts can, but we can't. This is a naval court, and we must obey naval law.

"There are men on this ship, and everywhere in the Navy, who didn't choose to be here. Do they want to fight? We don't know. They're in the Navy, so they fight for the King. We don't ask their opinion of the war. We give them orders. And there are men like them on the French ships. Some of those men are probably against the war. But they follow orders and they fight against our men.

"We don't ask our men what they think. And Budd's thoughts aren't important either." The captain looked at the three men again. "I know that you're worried about this," he said. "But we must act quickly because the enemy ships are near. We must decide now. Is Budd guilty or innocent?"

The sailing officer spoke for the first time. His voice was shaking. "Can we send him to prison if he's guilty? Or will he have to die?"

"If he's guilty, he must die," replied the captain. "That's the law. The men on this ship know that. We don't need to explain it to them. And we can't explain it to them. We're officers. They must follow our orders without thinking. Budd's crimes were murder and mutiny. We will tell the men that. They know the punishment.

"If Budd isn't punished, they'll ask 'why?' There'll be another mutiny. The men will think that we're afraid of them. We must obey the law and do the right thing. But try to understand me, my friends. I feel sorry for this unlucky boy, too. He will understand how we feel. And he will accept what the court decides."

The captain crossed the deck and looked out the window again. He waited for the three officers to decide. The men sat in worried silence.

"Captain Vere believes what he said," they thought. "But we

don't agree with everything. What can we do? We're naval officers, and he's our captain. Budd killed an officer at sea in wartime. And the punishment for that is death."

The court judged Billy Budd guilty. They decided to hang him early the next morning. Usually, a man is hanged immediately. But it was nighttime, so they had to wait.

Chapter 11   "The court has decided"

Captain Vere wanted to tell the prisoner. He went into the small room next to the courtroom and sent away the guard.

"The court has decided," he said to the prisoner. "You're guilty, and the punishment is hanging. It will happen in the morning."

We know that Captain Vere said these things. But what did he and the prisoner talk about after that? We don't know. But we know the two men, and we can imagine their conversation.

The captain didn't hide anything from Billy. He repeated what he said in the court. He gave his reasons, and he explained the law. He spoke to Billy about his punishment.

"He knows that I'm not afraid to die," thought Billy.

The captain really wanted Billy to understand. Billy was probably pleased about this, because a captain didn't usually talk to a sailor in that way.

The captain was a naval officer. On the outside, he seemed to be a hard man. But he was old enough to be Billy's father. Did he have strong feelings for Billy in his heart? We don't know.

The first lieutenant saw Captain Vere as he left the prisoner. There was a look of terrible pain on the captain's face. The prisoner's face was calm.

Many things happened in a very short time on that day. Claggart walked into the captain's cabin and he didn't leave it

The first lieutenant saw Captain Vere as he left the prisoner.

alive. When Billy left the cabin, he was a prisoner. He knew that his death was near.

In the next hour and a half, the men on the *Bellipotent* began to ask questions. "Why is the officer of the guard in the captain's cabin? And why is Billy Budd there, too?" asked one man.

"I don't know," said another. "I saw them go into the cabin. But they haven't come out." A ship is like a small town. Everybody knows what the others are doing.

Then the men were called on deck. This was unusual. It was nighttime and the weather was good. "Why are we here?" the men asked themselves. "Something's wrong. Where's Claggart? And where's Billy?"

A full moon shone as the men's shadows moved across the deck. Captain Vere stood with his officers. The guards stood up straight on both sides.

The captain spoke simply and clearly to his men, and he told them everything. "The officer of the guard is dead," he said. "He was killed by a topman called Billy Budd. We called a court immediately. The court decided that the prisoner is guilty. We will hang him early tomorrow morning."

He didn't use the word "mutiny," and he didn't tell the men to stay calm. It wasn't necessary. "They'll understand when they see his punishment," he thought.

The sailors stood silently and listened. When the captain finished, they began to speak. Their voices got louder. Then suddenly, the officers shouted an order. The men stopped talking, moved to their positions, and turned the ship around.

Claggart's body was given to some officers from his part of the ship. The officers and men came and stood on deck again. They watched as two men carefully lowered the body into the sea. They always did this when a man died at sea. They didn't do anything differently for Claggart.

And they didn't do anything differently for Billy. Everything happened in the usual way. Captain Vere didn't talk to Billy again after he left him in his cabin. The guards took Billy away. Nobody, except the chaplain, had permission to talk to him.

The guards watched Billy carefully. The officers watched the men carefully, but secretly. They didn't want the men to know. It was always like that when there was trouble on a ship.

Chapter 12   The Last Night

On a ship like the *Bellipotent*, the top gun deck was open to the weather. There were no beds there because the men slept on the lower gun decks. They also ate and kept their bags there.

A guard watched Billy as he lay on the deck between two cannon. They were big and heavy, and they had big wheels. Everything was painted black, the color of death. The sailor was wearing a dirty white shirt and pants. There were two smoky oil-burning lights over his head.

The Handsome Sailor lay quietly on the deck, thinking. His face was calm and he didn't move. His pain was gone now, after his talk with Captain Vere. Sometimes a little smile crossed his face. He was dreaming or remembering something.

When the chaplain came to him, Billy didn't notice him. The chaplain watched the young sailor for a minute, then went away. "He looks very calm," he thought. "He doesn't need me."

But he returned early in the morning. The prisoner saw him this time. He smiled and spoke to him politely.

"You're going to die this morning," said the chaplain. "Do you understand?"

Billy understood, and he talked freely about his death. He wasn't afraid. He was a simple man, and he never learned to fear death.

The *Bellipotent*'s chaplain was a kind man and he had a good heart. He talked about life and death. Billy listened politely, but he wasn't very interested.

"I'll leave him alone now," the good chaplain said to himself. "I know that he's a good man. The lieutenant told me all about him. He's innocent, so he doesn't need religion." Before he left, the chaplain did something unusual. He kissed the prisoner on the face. "I can't teach him anything now," he thought. "But I'm not worried about him."

Why didn't the chaplain try to save the innocent young sailor's life? Because he couldn't do anything. He, too, had to obey the laws of the Navy. The man of religion was paid by the men of war.

Chapter 13   The Next Morning

The moon shone brightly on the top decks, but it was dark below. As the night ended, a pale light shone through a cloud in the east. The light slowly became stronger.

It was four o'clock in the morning when the officers called the men onto the deck. It was time for the punishment.

Some of the men were already on deck because they were working there. Others came pouring out from the lower decks. Some of the younger sailors climbed up high into the sails. They wanted to see everything. The other men were crowded between the cannon. They waited silently or spoke softly.

The guards stood up straight in a square. Captain Vere stood in the middle, with his officers, and faced the front of the ship.

The prisoner arrived with the chaplain. Two sailors were waiting for him. They were standing under a spar in the middle of the ship. The men all noticed the chaplain. He spoke to the prisoner, and he acted very kindly.

The two sailors quickly put the rope around Billy's neck. The time was near. Billy faced the back of the ship.

Just before he was hanged, he spoke his last words. "Long live Captain Vere!" His voice was as clear and musical as a bird's.

The surprised men all replied at the same time, "Long live Captain Vere!" But they saw only Billy, and only Billy was in their hearts.

When he heard these words, Captain Vere stood very straight. His face showed no feelings.

When the last sign was given, the sunlight broke through a beautiful cloud in the east. Everyone watched as the rope pulled Billy's body up in the air. It stopped when it reached the spar. The first pink light of the morning shone on the hanged man.

Billy's body didn't move after it reached the spar. All of the men saw that and they were all surprised. Only the great ship continued to move slowly on the waves.

The ship's doctor and the ship's pilot walked back to their cabins together. "Did you see that?" the pilot asked the doctor. "The hanged man didn't move as he died. That shows a very strong mind, doesn't it?"

"What do you mean, Mr. Pilot?" asked the doctor. "Budd couldn't *decide* one way or the other." His voice was polite but impatient. "This was a scientific hanging. I told the men exactly what to do. They weighed the prisoner and they measured the rope. Then they put the right weight on the other end of the rope. Parts of the body do move when someone is hanged. But a dying man can't decide to stop that movement."

"But aren't there *always* small movements?" asked the pilot.

"Yes, there are, Mr. Pilot," replied the doctor.

"Then why weren't there any when *this* man was hanged?" continued the other man.

"Mr. Pilot, Budd was surely very afraid when the rope touched his neck. Maybe his heart suddenly stopped. Why didn't

"What does it mean?"

his arms and legs move after that? We don't know. It's strange, but we can't explain it."

The pilot continued. "But did he die of hanging? Or did he decide to die?"

"Decide to die?" said the doctor. "That idea comes from your imagination. It isn't scientific." He stood up to leave. "Excuse me, Mr. Pilot," he said. "I must go. A sick man is waiting for me. I don't want to leave him with my assistants."

There was complete silence on the ship for a minute or two after the hanging. The only sound was the waves that washed the sides of the ship. Then the men began to speak again. Their voices were quiet at first, but they became louder. It was an angry sound. Then there was a sudden order, and the silence returned. Half of the men returned to the lower decks. The other half returned to work.

When there is a serious crime on a warship, everything happens quickly. This time, the court was called immediately. They quickly found Billy Budd guilty, and he was hanged the next day. The sailmakers then put Billy's body into a sail with some heavy cannonballs. When they were ready, the officers called all the men back onto the deck.

They watched as Billy's body disappeared under the waves. There was the same sound of men's voices again. The voices were quiet but angry. And there was another sound this time. Some big seabirds saw Billy's body as it fell into the sea. They flew close to the ship, screaming. After the ship sailed away, they were still circling around Billy's final resting place. The men nervously watched the shadows of the birds and listened to their strange cries. "What does it mean?" they asked themselves.

Then another order was given and the men returned to their positions. They obeyed without thinking. Most of the men were on the gun decks. They stood by the cannon and waited. The first lieutenant stood in his place on deck, and the other lieutenants

Captain Vere fell to the deck.

made their reports to him. The first lieutenant repeated the reports to the captain.

These reports were made every day on the warship, but usually later—never at that time. Why did Captain Vere change the rules? Because he wanted to keep the men busy after Billy's death. He didn't want any trouble.

The band played some religious music. The chaplain spoke to the men. The warship was his church, and he spoke to the men every day. The band played again, then the men returned calmly to their places.

It was now daytime, and the clouds disappeared. The sky was clear and calm.

Chapter 14   The End of the Story

In a work of fiction, all the questions are answered at the end of the story. But this is a true story, so it can't be complete.

We have already heard the story of the Handsome Sailor in the year of the Great Mutiny, and his story ends with his death.

But our story doesn't finish there.

On the way back to the other English ships, the *Bellipotent* fought against a French ship. Captain Vere moved his ship next to the *Athée*. His sailors were preparing to climb onto the enemy ship when a gunshot came from the window of the French captain's cabin. Captain Vere fell to the deck, and his men carried him below.

The first lieutenant took the captain's place and won the fight. He took the ship back to join the English ships in Gibraltar.

Captain Vere and the other sick men were taken onto land. The captain lived for a few more days, but then the end came. He died before the great fight at Trafalgar, so he never became really famous. Did this matter to him? We can't be sure.

Before he died, they gave him drugs for his pain. He spoke his last words like a man in a dream: "Billy Budd, Billy Budd."

The doctor's assistant didn't understand this, but he repeated it to the first lieutenant. And he described the way that the captain said Billy's name. The captain wasn't sorry.

The first lieutenant didn't show his feelings about Billy's death. He never wanted Billy to die, but he couldn't say that now. He never talked to anybody about it.

A few weeks after the hanging, there was a story in the *News of the Mediterranean*, the Navy's newspaper. Some of the facts in the story were true, but some were not.

Here is the story:

"On the tenth of last month, a terrible thing happened on the warship *Bellipotent*. A sailor, William Budd, was planning trouble with some other men. Budd was caught by John Claggart, the officer of the guard, and Claggart took the man to see the captain. Suddenly, Budd pulled out a knife and cut open his heart.

"The crime and the knife show that the murderer was probably not English. Sometimes foreigners take English names. Our warships need men, so many foreign men join the Navy.

"This man is the worst kind of murderer; this was a terrible crime. The dead man was a fine man and an officer. His work on the ship was important and difficult. He did his work well and he loved his country.

"The murderer was immediately punished for his crime. This was a good lesson for the other men, and there will not be anymore trouble on the *Bellipotent*."

This story was written for a Navy newspaper that everyone has forgotten. But it is the only record of the lives of John Claggart and Billy Budd.

In the Navy, men have long memories. Sometimes, when they see a place or a thing, they remember a story. One example is the spar where Billy Budd was hanged. This spar was famous for a few years after his death. It moved from the ship to the shipyard, then back to the ship again. Finally, it stayed on land. The sailors always knew it when they saw it.

The sailors didn't know the secret facts of Billy's story. "The Navy had to punish him," they thought. But in their hearts, they didn't believe that he did wrong. "He wasn't planning a mutiny," they told themselves. "He wasn't like that, and he wasn't a murderer."

They remembered the Handsome Sailor's fresh young face. In their minds, he was always smiling from his heart. They had a romantic idea of the man and his mysterious death.

The men on the gun decks of the *Bellipotent* remembered the simple young man, too. One of the other topmen wrote a poem about him. The men passed the poem from one ship to another, then one man made it into a song. Billy Budd was gone but not forgotten.

ACTIVITIES

Chapters 1–4

Before you read

1 Find these words in your dictionary. They are all in the story. Then use them in the sentences below.

force innocent merchant mutiny Navy obey rights sea

Two hundred years ago, sailors didn't have many .... They were often taken from prisons or from ..... ships. Then they were ..... to join the .... These men went to ..... in warships and they had to ..... orders. Sometimes, there was a ..... on a warship. The Navy punished the men who started the trouble. Sometimes ..... men were punished, too.

2 Find these words in your dictionary.

cabin cannon captain corporal deck lieutenant stutter

Which words describe

a people in the Navy?

b things on a ship?

c a way of talking?

After you read

3 What are their names?

a the Handsome Sailor **e** the captain of the warship

b the merchant ship **f** the officer of the guard

c the captain of the merchant ship **g** the Danish sailor

d the warship **h** Longlegs

4 Discuss these questions about the story.

a How does Billy Budd join the Navy?

b What does Billy say when he leaves the merchant ship? Why? Why does the lieutenant shout at him?

c In 1767, thousands of English sailors refused to obey their officers' orders. Why?

d What is the job of the ship's corporals?

e Why does Billy go to see the old Danish sailor? What does Old Blue Smoke tell him? Why doesn't Billy believe him?

Chapters 5–9

Before you read

5 Chapter 5 is called "An Angry Man." Who is angry, do you think? Why? What will happen as a result?

6 What do the words in *italics* mean? Check in your dictionary.

    a He didn't say anything, but I saw *guilt* in his eyes.

    b She was *hanged* from a tree.

After you read

7 Answer these questions.

    a Why is Claggart angry when Billy drops his soup?

    b How does Claggart feel about Billy? Why?

    c Why does the watchman come to see Billy? What does Billy tell him?

    d What does Claggart tell Captain Vere?

    e Claggart repeats his story to Billy. What does Billy do? Why?

    f Why does the court meet secretly?

8 Work with another student. Have this conversation.
    Student A: You are Claggart. Tell Billy, "I know that you're planning a mutiny with other men. And I can prove it!"
    Student B: You are Billy Budd. Defend yourself.

Chapters 10–14

Before you read

9 What will the court decide? What do you think? Give reasons.

10 Find these words in your dictionary.

    chaplain   rope   spar

    Which word is it?

    a It is made of wood.   **b** It is a person.   **c** You can tie it.

After you read

11 Who says this?

    a "We need more information."

    b "I have nothing more to say, sir."

    c "We can't listen to our feelings."

    d "He wasn't planning a mutiny!"

    e "Long live Captain Vere!"

12 Are these right or wrong? Correct the mistakes.

    a The captain is calm when he leaves the prisoner.

    b The captain doesn't talk to the men about a mutiny.

    c The men are calm after the chaplain speaks to them.

    d The Navy's newspaper tells the true story of Billy Budd.

13 Discuss these questions. Why does the court decide that Billy is guilty? Do they make the right decision?

Writing

14 Describe John Claggart. What does he look like? What is he like? Is he popular on the warship? What is his part in this story?

15 What do you know about Captain Vere? Write about his life for a newspaper, after his death.

16 You are guarding Billy Budd on his last night. He wants to write a letter to a friend on the *Rights-of-Man*, but he cannot write. Write his words for him. Explain what has happened to him.

17 This story happens in 1797. What is different about a sailor's life today? What is the same?

Answers for the Activities in this book are published in our free resource packs for teachers, the Penguin Readers Factsheets, or available on a separate sheet. Please write to your local Pearson Education office or to: Marketing Department, Penguin Longman Publishing, 5 Bentinck Street, London W1M 5RN.